T0039788

WORLD'S FAVORITE MASTERWORKS FOR TRUMPET
Compiled by JAY ARNOLD

This volume contains some of the finest etudes ever written for the trumpet, combined with the complete works for orchestra. These trumpet parts may be used to great advantage for play-along study by working with records of these important compositions.

CONTENTS   **Page**

TWELVE ARTISTIC STUDIES

SAINT-JACOME

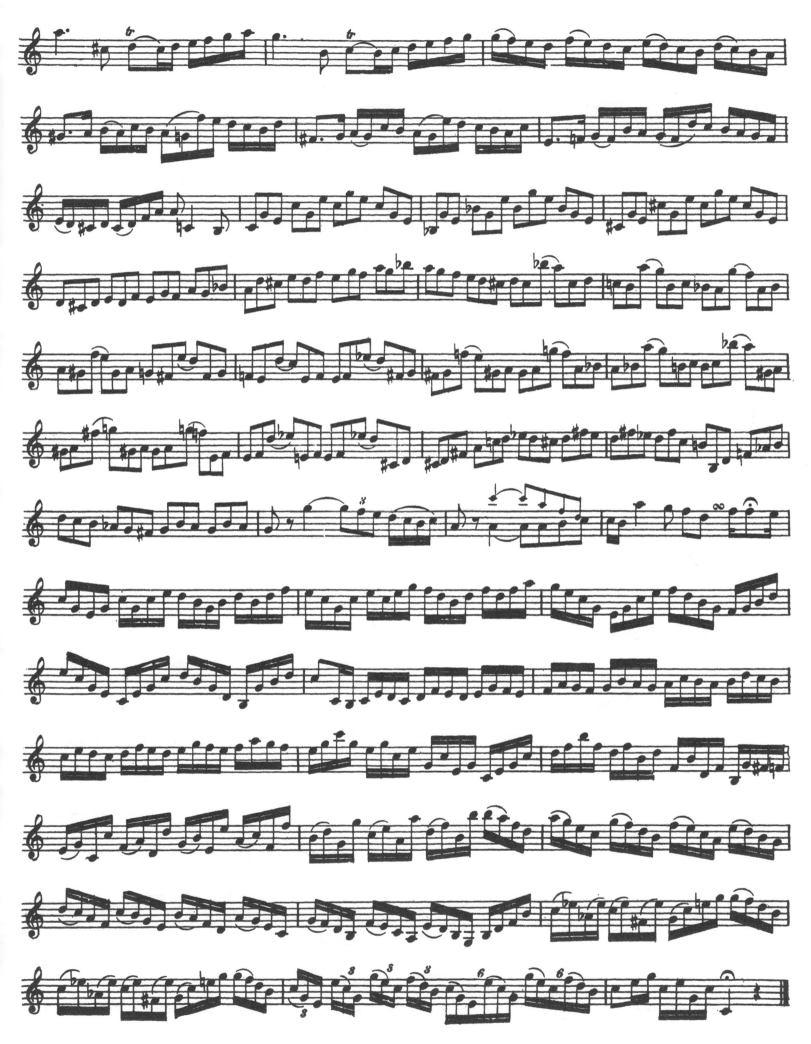

very moderate

8

Allegretto

4

Slower

9 Maestoso

10

Majore

Cantabile

24

Tempo

THIRTY-SIX STUDIES

N. BOUSQUET

Allegro moderato

Allegro moderato

Moderato

leggiero

dolce

a tempo
rit. *espressivo*

rit. *tr* *tr*

tr *tr* *tr* *tr*

cresc.

espress.

D. C.

Mouvement de Valse

Allegro moderato

8

Tempo di marcia

9

10 Allegretto

Moderato

11

Mouvement de Valse

Allegro moderato

13

Allegro moderato

14

44

15 Allegro moderato

Tempo I

Allegro moderato

17

Allegro moderato

19

Allegro moderato

20

Allegro

21

Allegro moderato

22

Allegro

23

The same in B♭ major, altering accidental ♯ to ♮, ♮ to ♭ and 𝄪 to ♯.

Moderato

24

cresc.

dim.

WALTZ TIME

Moderato

Allegro

25

Double tongueing

Andantino

26

Allegro moderato

28

Mouvement de Valse

29

Moderato

30

FIVE STUDIES

DOMENICO GATTI

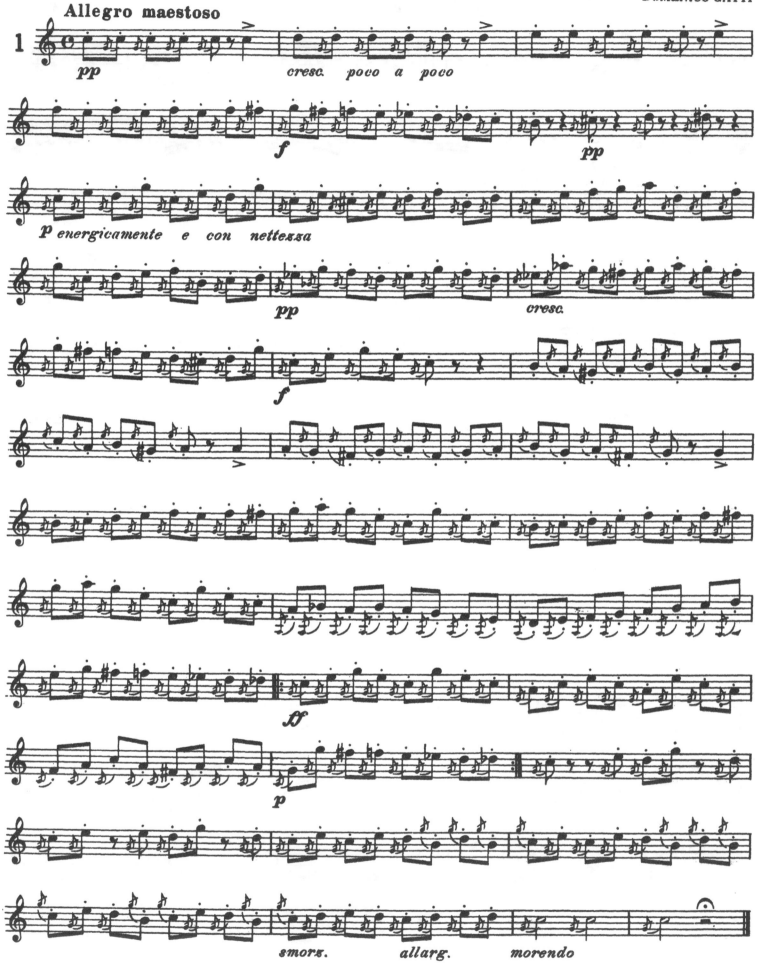

Allegro maestoso

smors.   allarg.   morendo

Adagio

3

Allegretto grazioso

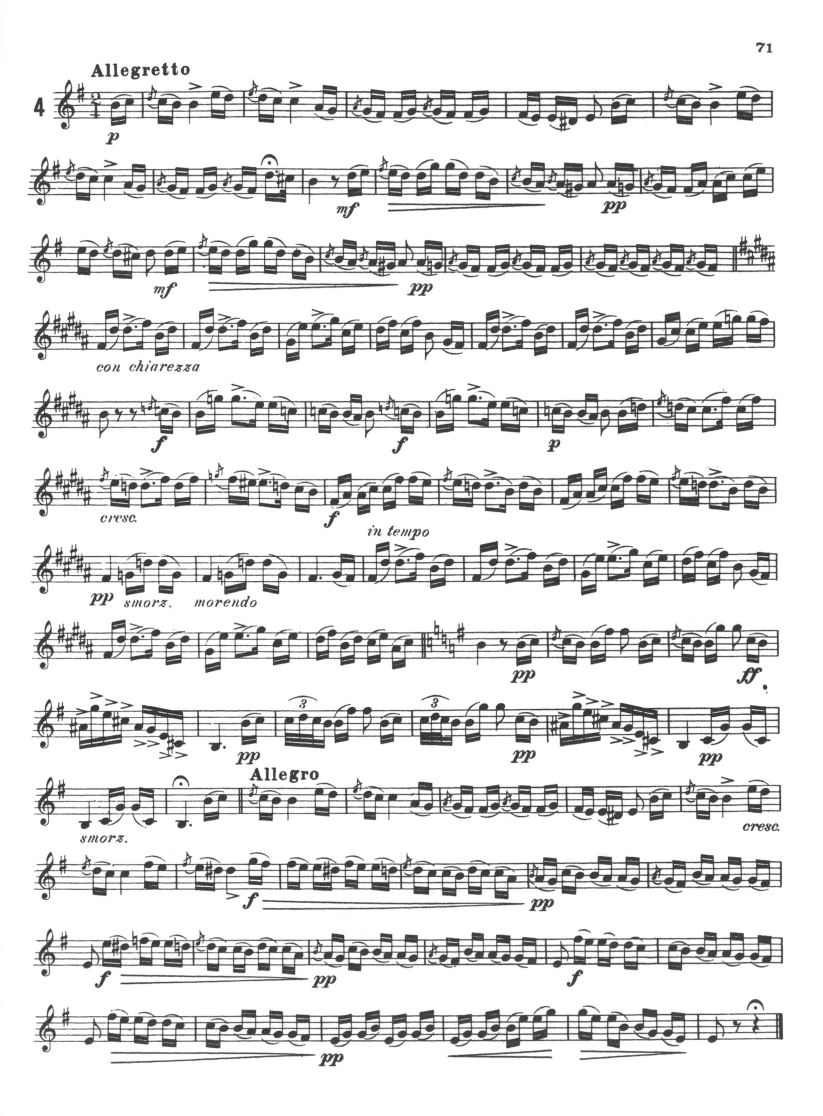

Allegretto appassionato

5

THIRTY-FOUR ETUDES

W. BRANDT

2

3

82

11

Leonora Signal

ff > > *rall.*

Alla Polacca

12

Marciale

13

Maestoso
marcato

14

Scherzando M.M. ♩ = 82.

15

a tempo

ril.

ad lib

Scherzando M. ♩.=126.

17

18

19 Allegro à la chasse M. ♪.=112

Allegretto

25

Vivo Vivace (Presto)

27

tu tu ku   tu tu ku   tu tu ku

1

(M. ♩=104)

28

tu ta ku tu tu ku tu ta ku tu tu tu ku

Scherzo

31

SUITE FROM THE OPERA

LE COQ D'OR

Tromba I in C

NICHOLAS RIMSKY-KORSAKOFF

III

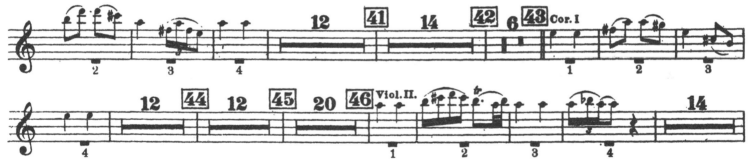

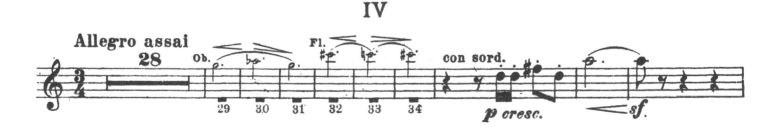

IV

Tromba I in C

Fine

SCHEHERAZADE

SYMPHONIC SUITE

Tromba I

NICHOLAS RIMSKY-KORSAKOFF, Op. 35

Tromba I

Tromba I
III

Tromba I

Tromba I

SYMPHONY NO. 4

I

TROMBA I in F

PETER I. TSCHAIKOWSKY, Op. 36

TROMBA I in F

TROMBA I in F

II

118

III SCHERZO PIZZICATO OSTINATO

TROMBA I in F

Scherzo D.C. al segno e poi la Coda

IV FINALE

TROMBA I in F

Allegro con fuoco

TROMBA I in F

Fine

SYMPHONY NO. 6

(PATHETIQUE)

TROMPETE I

PETER I. TSCHAIKOWSKY, Op. 74

TROMPETE I

TROMPETE I

III

TROMPETE I

TROMPETE I

IV
Finale